I0799090

A Blur with Fur

by Chris Mathews
illustrated by Mark Corcoran

Core Decodable 50

McGraw Hill Education

Bothell, WA • Chicago, IL • Columbus, OH • New York, NY

MHEonline.com

Copyright © 2015 McGraw-Hill Education

All rights reserved. No part of this publication may be reproduced or distributed in any form or by any means, or stored in a database or retrieval system, without the prior written consent of McGraw-Hill Education, including, but not limited to, network storage or transmission, or broadcast for distance learning.

Send all inquiries to:
McGraw-Hill Education
8787 Orion Place
Columbus, OH 43240

ISBN: 978-0-02-143449-7
MHID: 0-02-143449-2

Printed in Canada.

9 10 11 12 KOD 24

A blur with fur crossed the carpet.

A blur with fur ran and crossed the curb.

A blur with fur ran fast.

It turned a corner and left tracks in the grass.

The blur with fur dashed and crashed.
It curled and twirled.

What is that blur with fur?

It is Burt!

The blur with fur is Burt.